故園畫憶

庚寅中秋 韓磬沱 題

《故园画忆系列》编委会

名誉主任：韩启德

主　　任：邵　鸿

委　　员：(按姓氏笔画为序)

万　捷	王秋桂	方李莉	叶培贵
刘魁立	况　晗	严绍璗	吴为山
范贻光	范　芳	孟　白	邵　鸿
岳庆平	郑培凯	唐晓峰	曹兵武

故园画忆系列
Memory of the Old
Home in Sketches

粤北老风情
Historic Scenes of North Guangdong

曹秋艳　绘画 撰文
Sketches & Notes by Cao Qiuyan

学苑出版社
Academy Press

图书在版编目（CIP）数据

粤北老风情 / 曹秋艳绘画、撰文. — 北京：学苑出版社，2015.9

（故园画忆系列）

ISBN 978-7-5077-4863-5

Ⅰ. ①粤… Ⅱ. ①曹… Ⅲ. ①风俗习惯—介绍—广东省 Ⅳ. ①K892.465

中国版本图书馆CIP数据核字（2015）第212860号

出 版 人：	孟　白
责任编辑：	周　鼎　李　耕
出版发行：	学苑出版社
社　　址：	北京市丰台区南方庄2号院1号楼
邮政编码：	100079
网　　址：	www.book001.com
电子信箱：	xueyuanpress@163.com
联系电话：	010-67601101（营销部）、67603091（总编室）
经　　销：	全国新华书店
印 刷 厂：	北京信彩瑞禾印刷厂
开本尺寸：	889×1194 1/24
印　　张：	6.75
字　　数：	130千字
图　　幅：	133幅
版　　次：	2015年9月北京第1版
印　　次：	2015年9月北京第1次印刷
定　　价：	50.00元

目　　录

自序　　　　　　　　　　　　　曹秋艳

韶关市·曲江区、浈江区、南雄市

南华寺·石牌坊　　　　　　　　3
南华寺·石碑　　　　　　　　　4
南华寺·钟枕　　　　　　　　　5
南华寺·百年香炉　　　　　　　6
南华寺·莲花塔　　　　　　　　7
南华寺·墙　　　　　　　　　　8
苏拱门楼　　　　　　　　　　　9
文武阁塔　　　　　　　　　　　10
韶州府学宫　　　　　　　　　　11
风采楼（韶关市博物馆）　　　　12
骑楼（一）　　　　　　　　　　13
骑楼（二）　　　　　　　　　　14
北伐战争纪念馆　　　　　　　　15
中共粤北省委旧址　　　　　　　16
三影塔　　　　　　　　　　　　17
珠玑古巷　　　　　　　　　　　18
珠玑石塔　　　　　　　　　　　19
古城墙　　　　　　　　　　　　20
梅关关楼与古道　　　　　　　　21
新龙塔　　　　　　　　　　　　22
大塘上朔塔　　　　　　　　　　23
回龙寺塔　　　　　　　　　　　24
莲开净寺　　　　　　　　　　　25

七星世镇城堡　　　　　　　　　26
平林惜字塔　　　　　　　　　　27
篛过古村　　　　　　　　　　　28
坪田古村　　　　　　　　　　　29
新田村居民　　　　　　　　　　30
水西桥　　　　　　　　　　　　31
新田村·街巷　　　　　　　　　32
新田古村·照壁　　　　　　　　33

韶关市·乐昌市、乳源县、翁源县

应山古村·全景　　　　　　　　37
应山古村·民居（一）　　　　　38
应山古村·民居（二）　　　　　39
应山古村·飞檐　　　　　　　　40
应山石桥　　　　　　　　　　　41
户昌山村·全景　　　　　　　　42
户昌山村·建筑　　　　　　　　43
户昌山村·灰塑　　　　　　　　44
甘棠镇村　　　　　　　　　　　45
通济桥　　　　　　　　　　　　46
文昌塔　　　　　　　　　　　　47
文塔　　　　　　　　　　　　　48
云门寺　　　　　　　　　　　　49
云门寺·舍利塔　　　　　　　　50

观澜书院（一）	51
观澜书院（二）	52
必背瑶寨（一）	53
必背瑶寨（二）	54
八角塔	55
翁源八卦围（一）	56
翁源八卦围（二）	57
湖心坝客家群楼	58
湖心坝客家群楼（二）	59
湖心坝客家群楼（三）	60
葸茅围	61
古民居石雕	62

韶关市·仁化县、始兴县、新丰县

普同塔	65
东庄门楼	66
云龙寺塔	67
石塘村	68
石塘村·民居（一）	69
石塘村·民居（二）	70
石塘村民居·古巷	71
石塘村民居·高墙	72
石塘村民居·大门	73
石塘村·祠堂（一）	74
石塘村·祠堂（二）	75
石塘村·祠堂（三）	76
双峰寨	77
双峰寨·侧面	78

双峰寨·内部	79
丹霞山（一）	80
丹霞山（二）	81
周所塔	82
广州会馆	83
满堂客家大围	84
满堂客家大围·民居（一）	85
满堂客家大围·民居（二）	86
满堂客家大围·内部	87
满堂客家大围·天井	88
满堂客家大围·灰塑	89
东湖坪村·祠堂	90
东湖坪民俗文化村	91
东湖坪民俗文化村·牌坊	92
东湖坪民俗文化村·永成堂围楼	93
东湖坪民俗文化村·灰塑	94
九栋十八井（一）	95
九栋十八井（二）	96

清远市·连州市、英德市、佛冈县、清新县

丰阳古村（一）	99
丰阳古村（二）	100
白鹤寨	101
白家城	102
慧光塔	103
洪秀全传教屋	104
丰溪古庙	105

卿罡古村	106		瑶族·耍歌堂	127
彭家祠（一）	107		瑶族·舞蹈	128
彭家祠（二）	108		南华诞	129
蓬莱寺塔	109		采茶戏	130
老地湾	110		石塘月姐歌	131
林公祠	111		高桥舞狮	132
赵氏宗祠	112		双龙舞双狮	133
上岳古村（一）	113		十点梅花	134
上岳古村（二）	114		舞纸马	135
上岳古村（三）	115		舞春牛	136
上岳古村（四）	116		乐昌三溪青蛙狮	137
乾隆皇家大院	117		鹤蚌舞	138
七星岗塔	118		粤剧	139
清远楼	119		仁化土法造纸	140
故乡里民俗文化主题公园	120		剪纸	141

民风民俗

			客家人婚俗	142
瑶族·刺绣	123		客家·回娘家	143
瑶族·反面刺绣	124		张田饼印	144
瑶族·小长鼓舞	125		趟栊门	145
瑶族·长鼓舞	126		客家·石磨	146
			打谷子	147

Contents

Preface   Cao Qiuyan

Shaoguan City · Qujiang District, Zhenjiang Distrct, Nanxing City

Nanhua Temple	3
Nanhua Temple • Stone Tablet	4
Nanhua Temple • Zhongzhen	5
Nanhua Temple • Hundred-Year-Old Incense Burner	6
Nanhua Temple • Lotus Pagoda	7
Nanhua Temple • Walls	8
Sugong Gateway	9
Wenwuge Tower	10
Shaozhou Institute (Shaozhou Confucian Temple)	11
Fengcai Building (Shaoguan Museum)	12
The Arcade (1)	13
The Arcade (2)	14
Memorial Hall of the Northern Expedition	15
Former Site of North Guangdong Provincial Committee of the Chinese Communist Party	16
Sanying Pagoda	17
Zhuji Historic Alley	18
Stone Tower of Zhuji	19
Ancient City Walls	20
Meiguan Pass Tower and Ancient Meiguan Pass Road	21
Xinlong Tower	22
Datang Shangsuo Tower	23
Huilong Temple Pagoda	24
Liankaijing Temple	25
Qixingshizhen Castle	26
Pinglin Xizi Tower	27
Ruoguo Old Village	28
Pingtian Old Village	29
Xintian Village	30
Shuixi Bridge	31
Xintian Village • Alleys	32
Xintian Old Village • Screen Walls	33

Shaoguan City · Lechang City, Ruyuan County, Wengyuan County   35

Yingshan Historic Village	37
Yingshan Historic Village • Residence (1)	38
Yingshan Historic Village • Residence (2)	39
Yingshan Historic Village • Flying Ridges	40
Yingshan Stone Bridge	41
Huchangshan Village	42
Huchangshan Village • Buildings	43
Huchangshan Village • Plaster Engravings	44
Gantangzhen Village	45
Tongji Bridge	46
Wenchang Tower	47
Wen Tower	48
Yunmen Temple	49
Yunmen Temple • Sharia Pagoda	50
Guanlan Academy (1)	51
Guanlan Academy (2)	52

Bibei Yao Village (1)	53
Bibei Yao Village (2)	54
Bajiao Tower	55
Eight-Diagram Shaped Building in Wengyuan (1)	56
Eight-Diagram shaped Building in Wengyuan (2)	57
Hakka Building Complex, Huxinba	58
Hakka Building Complex, IIuxinba (2)	59
Hakka Building Complex, Huxinba (3)	60
Simaowei	61
Stone Engraving of Historic House Relics	62

Shaoguan City · Renhua County, Shixing County, Xinfeng City

Putong Tower	65
Dongzhuang Gateway	66
Yunlong Temple Pagoda	67
Shitang Village	68
Shitang Village • Civilian Residence (1)	69
Shitang Village • Civilian Residence (2)	70
Civilian Residence in Shitang Village • Old Alleys	71
Civilian Residence in Shitang Village • High Walls	72
Civilian Residence in Shitang Village • Front Door	73
Shitang Village • Ancestral Temple (1)	74
Shitang Village • Ancestral Temple (2)	75
Shitang Village • Ancestral Temple (3)	76
Shuangfeng Village	77
Shuangfeng Zhai • Side	78
Shuangfeng Stockade • Interior Scene	79
Mount Danxia (1)	80
Mount Danxia (2)	81
Zhousuo Tower	82
Guangzhou Hall	83
Mantang Hakka Manor	84
Hakka Walled Houses • Residence (1)	85
Hakka Walled Houses • Residence (2)	86
Mantang Hakka Manor • Interior Scene	87
Hakka Walled House • Patio	88
Hakka Walled House • Plaster Engravings	89
Donghuping Village • Ancestral Temple	90
Donghuping Folk Culture Village	91
Donghuping Folk Culture Village • Memorial Gateway	92
Donghuping Folk Culture Village • Yongchengtang Walled House	93
Donghuping Folk Culture Village • Plaster Engraving	94
Nine-Buildings-Eighteen-Patios (1)	95
Nine-Buildings-Eighteen-Patios (2)	96

Qingyuan City · Lianzhou City, Yingde City, Fogang City, Qinxin County

Fengyang Historic Village (1)	99
Yangfeng Historic Village (2)	100

Baihe Village	101
Baijiacheng Village	102
Huiguang Tower	103
Missionary House, Hong Xiuquan	104
Fengxi Old Temple	105
Qinzhen Old Village	106
Peng Clan Academy (1)	107
Peng Clan Academy (2)	108
Penglai Temple Pagoda	109
Laodi Bay	110
Lin Clan Ancestral Temple	111
Zhao Clan Academy	112
Shangyue Historic Village (1)	113
Shangyue Historic Village (2)	114
Shangyue Historic Village (3)	115
Shangyue Historic Village (4)	116
Empire Courtyard of Qianlong	117
Qixinggang Tower	118
Qingyuan Building	119
Guxiangli Folk Culture Theme Park	120

Folk Customs

Yao Minority • Embroidery	123
Yao Minority • "Opposing" Embroidery	124
Yao Minority • Little Long Drum Dance	125
Yao Minority • Long Drum Dance	126
Yao Minority • Shuage tang Festival	127
Yao Minority • Dance	128
Nanhua Birthday Celebration	129
Tealeaf Picking Opera	130
Yuejie Song in Shitang	131
Bi-dragon and Bi-lion Dance	133
Shidian Meihua	134
Paper Horse Dance	135
Spring Bull Dance	136
Frog-and-Lion in Sanxi, Lechang	137
Crane and Clam Dance	138
Yue Opera	139
The Old Way of Paper-Making in Renhua	140
Paper Cutting	141
Hakka Wedding Customs	142
Hakka House • Coming Back to Mother's	143
Zhangtian MoonCake Moulds	144
Tanglong Door	145
Hakka House • Stone Mill	146
Thrashing	147

自　序

粤北，即广东省北部地区，通常指韶关、清远两个地级市下辖区域。粤北地区有悠久的历史，是广府民系南迁的重要中转站，也是客家民系形成与发展的重地。

韶关，古称韶州，是"马坝人"的故乡，石峡文化的发祥地，有着2100多年的历史。历史上的韶州被誉为"岭南名郡"，孕育了大批历史名人。佛教禅宗六祖惠能在韶州弘法37年，南华寺因此成为禅宗的"南宗祖庭"。源远流长的历史造就了韶关良好的人文环境。韶关作为中国优秀旅游城市、国家园林城市，是中国最具特色魅力城市之一。

清远，别称凤城，是一座年轻而充满魅力的城市。它是珠江三角洲开放地区和粤北山区政治、经济、文化交流的主要汇集区之一，也是广东省面积最大的地级市和少数民族主要聚居地。

2012年，经学苑出版社周鼎编辑的推荐，我有了参与绘制"故园画忆系列"书籍的机会。希望可以通过《故园画忆·粤北老风情》与更多人分享粤北的古城、古村、古民居和当地的风土人情，另一方面，也希望能够将特色的建筑文化展现出来。

本书的内容分为两部分，传统建筑是第一部分，也是篇幅最多的部分，其中按粤北地区的十三个辖区县市来具体描述，将各个区域的古建筑和民居都集中表现在一起了，青砖灰瓦、马头墙、客家围屋、瑶寨、佛塔寺庙、古村落，等等。第二部分是粤北地区保留至今的名俗特色活动，这些民俗中很多被列为国家非物质文化遗产，其中我们最熟悉的广东大戏——粤剧、采茶戏、祁剧等。还有民间习俗包括舞春牛、舞纸马、舞龙舞狮等在春节或元宵等节日里助兴祈福的活动。通过客观叙述和速写表现，能够使读者从一个侧面了解粤北地区历史、民族构成、建筑特征、宗教信仰、人民生活习惯等各方面信息。

本书完成之际，特别感谢那些帮助我的人们：学苑出版社，为我提供了编写出版的机会；我的学生，他们给了我很多有益的意见和建议。感谢我的家人、朋友和一切帮助我的人。

曹秋艳
2013 年 12 月

Preface

Yuebei, the northern part of Guangdong Province, usually refers to regions of Shaoguan and Qingyuan. Yuebei has a long history and is the most important for the development of Hakka culture.

Shaoguan, also named Shaozhou in old times, is the birthplace of the Maba people and origin of the 2,100-year-old Shixia culture. In Chinese history, Shaozhou was called the Famous County in Lingnan because many celebrities came from there. Huineng, the Sixth Patriarch of Chan Buddhism lived and taught there for 37 years; thus, Nanhua Temple became Home to South Zen. This lengthy history nourished the splendid cultural environment of Shaoguan.

Qingyuan, nicknamed Phoenix City, is the economic center of the Pearl River Delta area, the largest city at prefecture-level and a major settlement for minorities.

For this book some old cities, old civilian houses and some local customs in northern part of Guangdong are selected as representatives of Hakka culture in the hope of introducing the architecture and customs of northern Guangdong.

This book explores the traditional architecture including types of old structures and dwellings in different regions such as brick and tile, horsehead walls, Hakka walled houses, Yao village houses, Buddhist pagodas and temples, ancient villages, etc. In addition, some special cultural activities such as Yue Opera, Tealeaf Picking Opera, and Qi Opera and Dance of Spring Bull, Dance of Paper-horse, Dragon and Lion Dances are also introduced.

I express my appreciation to all those who helped make this book possible, especially the Academy Press editors, my students, my family and friends.

Cao Qiuyan
December, 2013

韶关市 · 曲江区、浈江区、南雄市
Shaoguan City · Qujiang District, Zhenjiang Distrct, Nanxing City

南华寺·石牌坊

原名南华禅寺，始建于北魏景明三年（502年），位于曲江区马坝镇。由曹溪门、放生池、宝林门、天王殿、大雄宝殿、藏经阁、灵照塔、六祖殿等建筑群组成。

Nanhua Temple

Built in 502 in Maba Town, Qujiang District, the temple mainly consists of captivity-freeing pond, Heavenly King Hall, Grand Hall, Sutra Depository, Lingzhao Pagoda and other Buddhist buildings.

南华寺·石碑

此碑"天王殿"外的石碑,神功圣德碑,记载"真龙天子"生前一世所做功德。一共有九个塑像,象征着神兽龙的九子。

Nanhua Temple · Stone Tablet

The nine carvings on the tablet, symbolize Shenshoulong's nine sons.

南华寺·钟枕

　　钟枕为鱼梆、龙头、鱼身中空的木鱼，一般挂在大雄宝殿的东庑廊下，敲击以通知粥饭时刻。

Nanhua Temple · Zhongzhen

Zhongzhen, a hollow wooden fish with a dragon head and watchman's clapper, is hung above Dongwu corridor in Grand Hall and struck, to announce meal times.

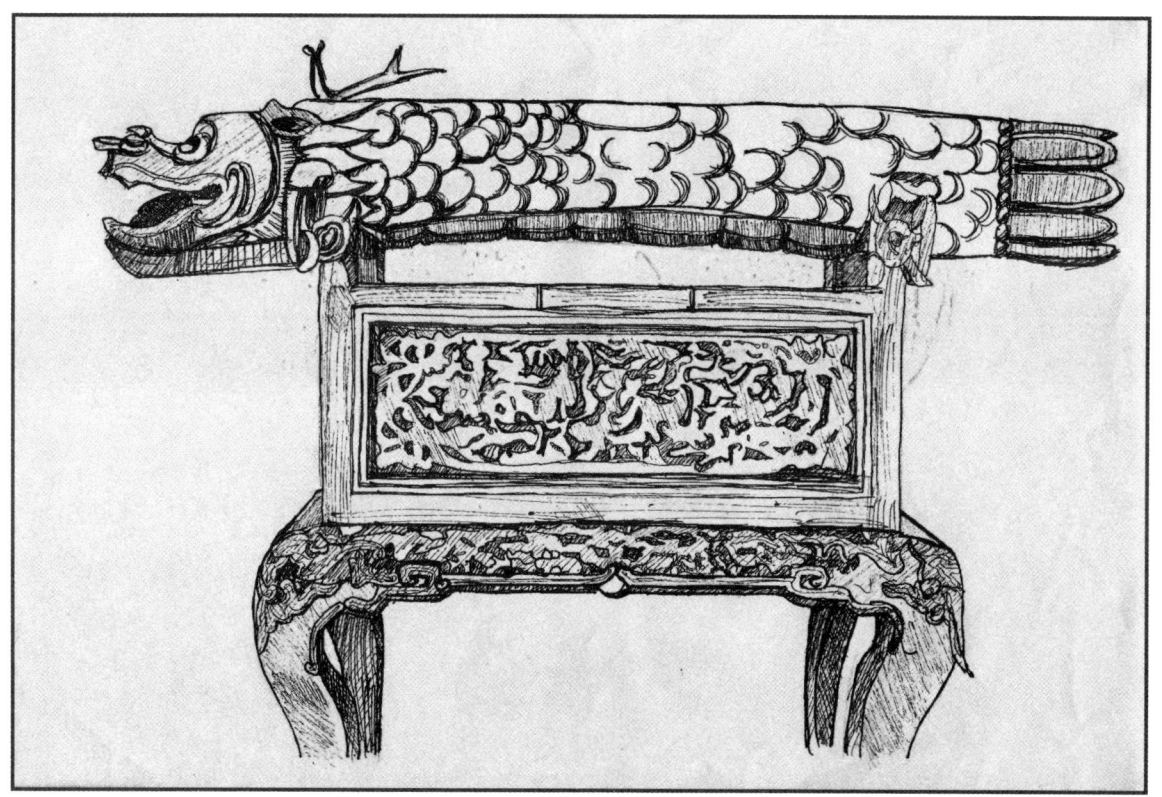

南华寺·百年香炉

此香炉由纯铜铸成，造型防建筑屋檐飞起，上有四只小神兽龙挂钟组成，发出清脆的声音。

Nanhua Temple · Hundred-Year-Old Incense Burner

This pure copper incense burner, shaped like the flying ridge of a house, with four little Shenshoulongs hung above the incense burner, gives a clear, melodious sound.

南华寺·莲花塔

此塔以莲花为基座,塔身仿舍利塔形式,屹立在百年南华寺中。

Nanhua Temple · Lotus Pagoda

This Sharia shaped pagoda on a lotus base, stands in the hundred-year-old Nanhua Temple yard.

{ 南华寺·墙 }

　　南华寺中整体建筑处处都体现了岭南园林建筑的特色，例如其墙头的屋檐翘角。

Nanhua Temple • Walls

Nanhua temple features Lingnan garden architecture with cornices and ridges on the wall tops.

苏拱门楼

建于宋代，位于曲江区白土镇。为牌坊式门楼，红沙岩为柱，中间楼顶悬山式，二层两边为歇山顶，六层砖出檐，檐下水磨砖作斗拱。

Sugong Gateway
Built during the Song Dynasty (960~1279), in Baitu Town, Qujjang District, the gateway has red sandstone columns with overhanging gable roof in the middle gate and gable and hip roof on both sides.

文武阁塔

建于清代，位于武江区龙归镇。六角五层楼阁式空心塔，青砖结构，内外墙面用石灰浆批荡，塔门正西向，券顶，石灰岩条石砌筑。

Wenwuge Tower

Built during the Qing Dynasty in Longgui Town, Wujiang District, the five-storey hexagonal hollow tower is made of black brick. The limestone gate has an arched roof.

韶州府学宫

即韶州孔庙，始建于北宋景德三年（1006年），明代重建，位于浈江区风采路。该殿筑高台上，前后檐柱置斗栱，上檐有九攒五踩斗栱，下檐施七踩斗栱。

Shaozhou Institute (Shaozhou Confucian Temple)

Built in 1006, restored during the Ming Dynasty, and located on Fengcai Road, Zhenjiang District, this temple was built on a high base.

风采楼（韶关市博物馆）

始建于明弘治年间（1488~1505年），位于浈江区风采路，高22米，正方形，顶为三重飞檐翘角，正中有华饰小圆顶，韶关市的标志性建筑，现为韶关市博物馆。

Fengcai Building (Shaoguan Museum)

This building, the symbol of Shaoguan, was built between 1488 and 1505 on Fengcai Road, Zhenjiang District. The square building, 22 meters tall, has three-levels of flying ridges on the top.

骑楼（一）

该骑楼位于韶关东堤中路附近，沿街部分用立柱支撑，陆上的楼为骑楼，临江一面是吊脚楼。

The Arcade (1)

Located near Dongti Road in Shaoguan City, the arcade is partly supported by columns beside the shops and stores. The complex includes the buildings on the land and waterfront building by the river.

骑楼（二）

楼层正面墙上并排开着两至三扇窗，立面基本无装饰。立面以垂直构图为主，设有哥特式门窗，底层骑楼廊也处理为仿哥特式窗形式。

The Arcade (2)

There are several Gothic windows in the front wall. In the arcade the corridor windows and the doors are also Gothic-like.

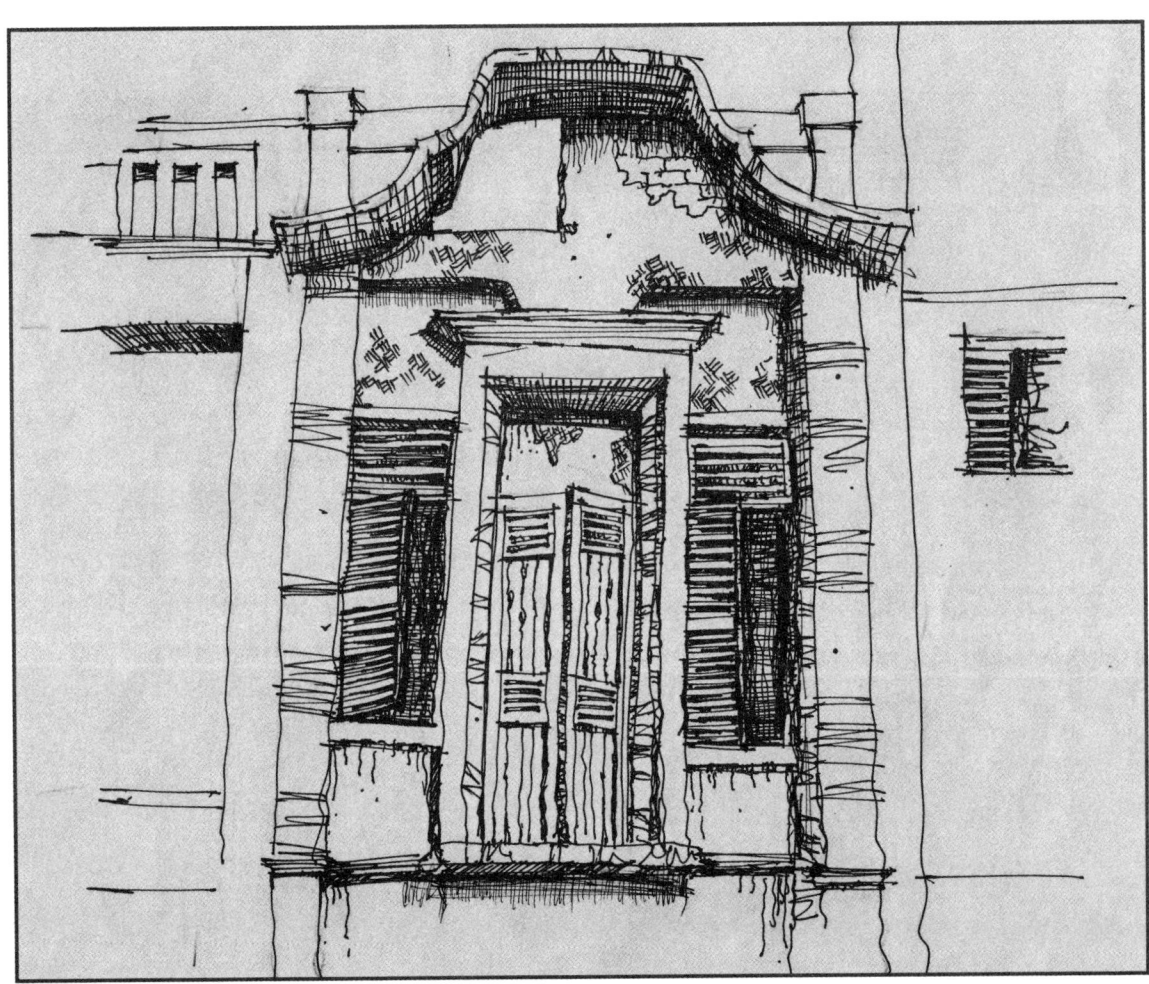

北伐战争纪念馆

建于2008年，位于浈江区帽子峰。为二层西式四合院砖木结构楼房，内设方形天井，钢筋混凝土框架，外墙为仿古青砖清水墙砌筑。

Memorial Hall of the Northern Expedition

Built in 2008, in Maozifeng, Zhenjiang District, the two-storey quadrangle courtyard is made with bricks and wood; square patio within and the outer walls are of black bricks and drywall.

中共粤北省委旧址

位于浈江区十里亭。中共粤北省委旧址长期作为韶关市乳制品厂办公场所、库房使用，内部进行改造对原有结构有一定的破坏。

Former Site of North Guangdong Provincial Committee of the Chinese Communist Party

After 1949, this building located in Zhenjiang, Shenjing District became factory offices and storage.

三影塔

原名延祥寺塔,建于宋大中祥符二年(1009年),位于南雄市永康路。塔身每层均伸出飞檐和栏杆,飞檐的梁头上都悬挂着一只铜钟,而檐脊上蹲伏着陶制貔貅。

Sanying Pagoda

Built in 1009, on Yongkang Road in Nanxiong City, the pagoda's flying ridges and railings extend out of each storey, with a bronze clock hanging on it and a porcelain Pixiu crouching on the ridges.

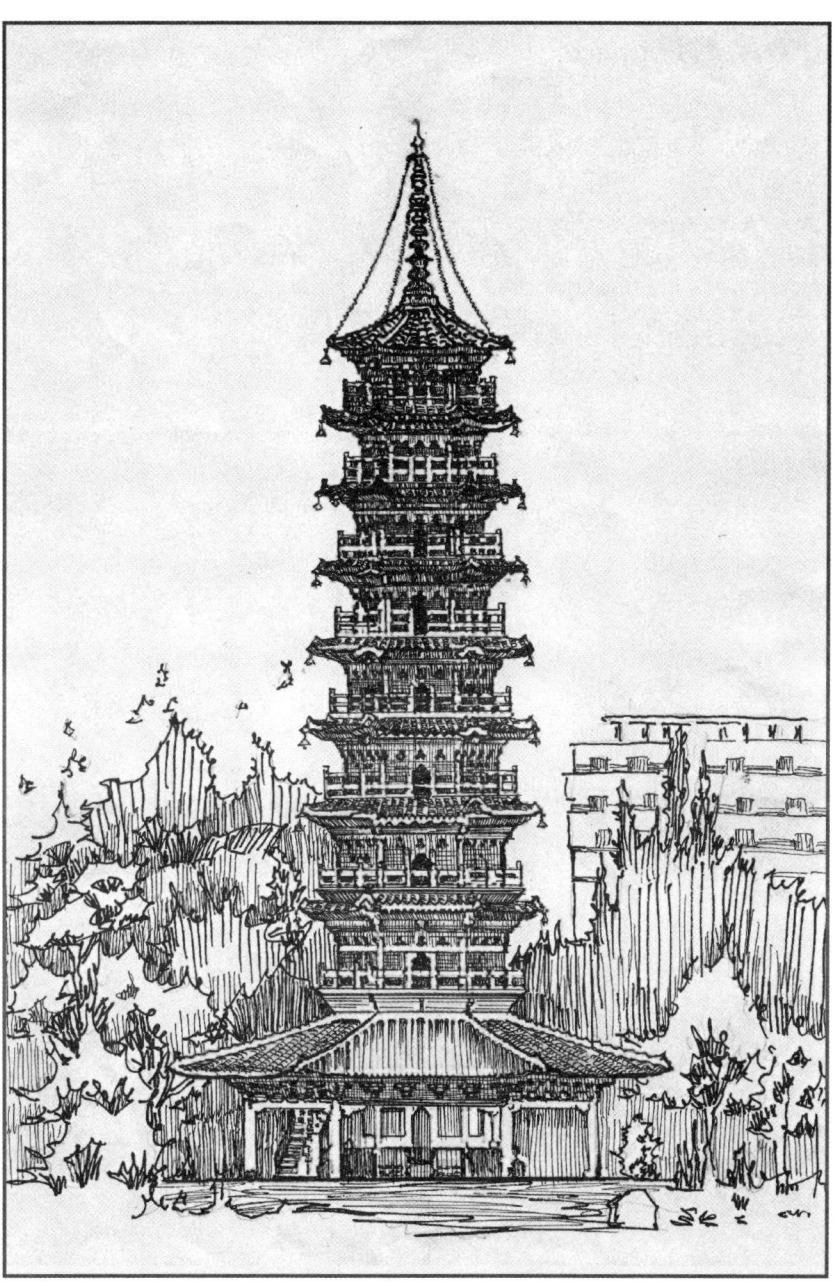

珠玑古巷

原名敬宗巷,位于南雄梅关古驿道上,具有1100多年历史。全长1500多米,全部用鹅卵石铺砌,两旁为民宅祠堂、店铺商号,有"广东第一巷"之誉。

Zhuji Historic Alley

The 1,100-year-old courier road in Meiguan, Nanxiong, is 1,500 meters long. It is known as the First Alley of Guangdong. Paved with cobblestones, the alley is lined with houses, ancestral temples and stores.

【珠玑石塔】

又名"贵妃塔",建于元至正十年(1350年),位于南雄珠玑古巷内。塔为八角七层实心幢式石塔,高3.4米,全塔共用17块红色砂质岩雕刻成形后垒叠而成,是广东省唯一有准确纪年的石塔。

Stone Tower of Zhuji

Built in 1350, the tower is in the old alley in Zhuji, Nanxiong. Built of stone, the hexagonal, seven-storey tower is 3.4 meters high. Seventeen red sandy rocks were engraved and shaped before fitted together here. Unique among stone towers in Guangdong, its construction date is known.

古城墙

时称斗城，建于宋皇祐四年（1052年），为南雄有城之始。扩建后城墙周长3770米，面积达1.13平方千米。新老城共设有16个圆拱型城门，在每个城门之上均建楼阁。

Ancient City Walls

Built in 1052, during the Song Dynasty, it is popularly known as Dou City. It was an original structure of Nanxiong City. It encompasses an area of 1.13sq kilometers. Along its 3,770-meter-perimeter are 16 domed gates with pavilions.

梅关关楼与古道

始建于秦汉，位于距南雄市梅岭。路面用青石块或鹅卵石铺砌，现存关楼和古道为明代遗物，关楼建在古道隘口分水岭南 20 米处，砖石结构。

Meiguan Pass Tower and Ancient Meiguan Pass Road

Built during the Qin and Han Dynasties (221B.C-220A.D), the Tower and ancient road are in Meiling Mountain, Nanxiong City. Paved with black stone bricks and cobblestones, the existing tower and ancient road are Ming Dynasty (1368-1644) relics.

新龙塔

建于宋代，位于南雄市坪田镇，为平面六角形楼阁式五层空心砖塔，塔刹已毁，残高 18 米。塔身砖砌阑额、角柱、斗拱，各层以菱角砖和拔檐砖叠涩出檐。

Xinlong Tower

Built during the Song Dynasty (960-1279), this tower is in Pingtian Town, Nanxiong City. The five-storey hexagonal tower was built with hollow bricks. The Tasha of the tower had been destroyed. The tower remnant is 18 meters high.

大塘上朔塔

建于清代,位于南雄市油山镇。为平面六角形楼阁式七层空心塔,高 19.9 米,各层用菱角砖和拔檐砖叠涩出檐,塔刹为葫芦形。造型规整,使外观显得稳重美观。

Datang Shangsuo Tower

Built during the Qing Dynasty (1644-1912), this elegant, hexagonal, 7-storey tower, built of hollow bricks, in Youshan Town, Nanxiong City, is 19.9 meters tall.

回龙寺塔

建于宋代，位于南雄市湖口镇。为平面六角形七层仿楼阁式空心砖塔，现存四层，残高16米。塔身均置砖砌斗拱、柱、阑额和普柏枋。

Huilong Temple Pagoda

Built during the Song Dynasty, the pagoda is in Hukou Town, Nanxiong City. The seven-storey hexagonal pavilion-like pagoda was built of hollow bricks. Only four stories remain with a height of 16 meters.

> 莲开净寺

原名莲社庵,始建于明代,1996年重建,位于南雄市南郊。继承了仿宋古建筑风格和佛教文化特征,采用四进三院式的布局。

Liankaijing Temple

Built during the Ming Dynasty, and rebuilt in 1996, it is located in southern suburb of Nanxiong City. The four-entrance, three-courtyard temple has Song Dynasty and Buddhist architectural styles.

七星世镇城堡

建于明嘉靖（1549年），位于南雄乌迳镇。该城平面呈椭圆形，门楼为布瓦歇山顶，正脊中央泥塑一圆形宝珠，梁架为穿斗式结构。该城只设一条拱形城门，用麻石和青砖砌筑。

Qixingshizhen Castle

Built in 1549, it is located in Wujing Town, Nanxiong City. The castle is oval-shaped castle, as a gate-tower covered by Buwa, mission roofing tiles, and Xieshanding hip and gable roof. The single arch gate is paved with granite and black bricks.

平林惜字塔

建于明代，位于南雄市油山镇。为平面六角形三层楼阁式空心砖塔，高7.2米，塔首层南北两面开一小门。该塔造型精巧，别具一格，保存较好。

Pinglin Xizi Tower

This three-storey hollow brick hexagonal tower, delicately designed and well-preserved, built during the Ming Dynasty in Youshan Town, Nanxiong City, is 7.2 meters tall.

鹅过古村

　　始建于南宋皇佑元年（1253年），距今已有761年的历史，是南雄久负盛名的书香之村，村中众多的人文历史遗迹，有古代书房、宗祠等多处古建筑。

Ruoguo Old Village

First built in 1253, it was the famous scholarly village in Nanxiong City with many historic relics, including ancient private studies, family academies, etc.

坪田古村

坪田镇是南粤有名的"银杏之乡",境内目前有百年以上树龄的古银杏树 5000 多株,年产白果数百吨。每年金秋古银杏树上树叶落黄,"银杏染秋"成为南雄秋冬时节一景。

Pingtian Old Village

Pingtian Town is the well-known Ginkgo Village, with 5,000 hundred-year-old ginkgo trees, which yields hundreds of tons of ginkgo nuts every year. During late autumn days when the old ginkgo tree leaves turn to yellow, they create the most beautiful seasonal scenesin Nanxiong.

新田村居民

建于西晋建兴三年（315年），位于南雄乌迳镇。古村内最引人注目的是唐宋元明清五朝的古民居，多为客家建筑，青墙玄瓦、凤头檐角、错落有致。

Xintian Village

Founded in 315 in Wujing Town, Nanxiong, the old village features old houses from the Tang, Song, Yuan, Ming and Qing dynasties, most of which are Hakka style with grey walls and red tiles with phoenix ridges and edges.

水西桥

又名万年桥,建于明万历年间(1573~1620年),清嘉庆十二年(1807年)重修,位于南雄水西村。为七墩八孔石筑平桥,整座桥为红色岩石砌成,东西向,桥上置石栏杆。

Shuixi Bridge

Built between 1573 and 1620 and remodeled in 1807, the bridge is in Shuixi Village, Nanxiong City. The seven-pier flat bridge with stone railings is made of red granite.

新田村·街巷

　　历史上的经济中心和物质集散地，附近的农民都会到此赶集，市场商贸繁华，街巷的走向、形态没有太多规律性和礼法限制。

Xintian Village • Alleys

Historically it was the economical and agricultural market center. Peasants from nearby areas still hold market here.

新田古村·照壁

新田村照壁造型各异，一般为天井照壁，中心铺方格纹砖，底部泥塑仙草鱼纹图。

Xintian Old Village • Screen Walls

The screen walls in Xintian old village are of various shapes and types. They are mostly patio screen walls, with squared brick in the middle and clay sculptures of mesona (a Chinese herb plant) and fish carved at the bottom.

韶关市·乐昌市、乳源县、翁源县
Shaoguan City · Lechang City, Ruyuan County, Wengyuan County

| 应山古村·全景 |

建于明永乐五年（1407年），位于乐昌黄圃镇。民居有上百栋，布局非常合理，前后分九排，每排九栋，每二栋或三栋相连，也有独建的"单脚"屋。

Yingshan Historic Village

Built in 1407, Huangpu Town, Lechang County has hundreds of buildings in nine rows, each row nine building; some semi-detach houses while others are detach homes.

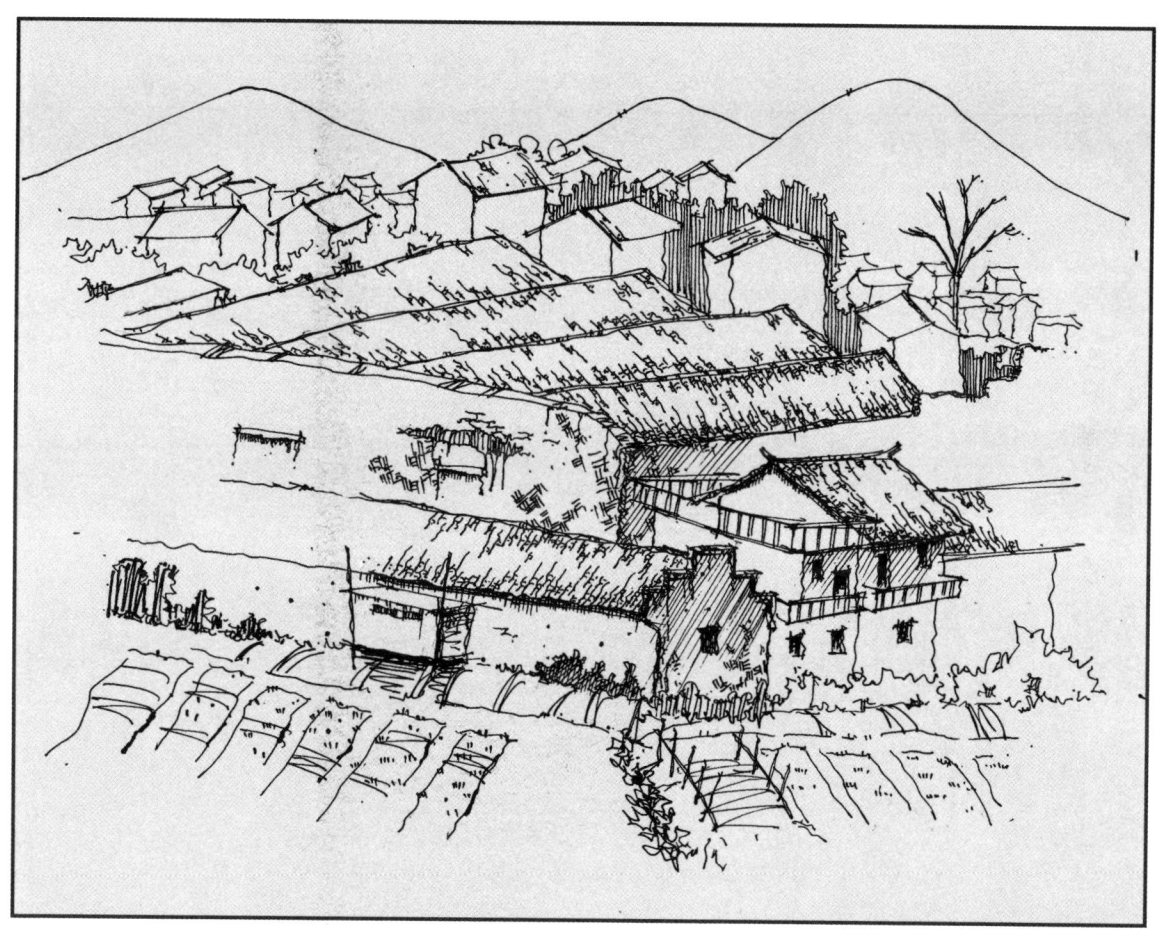

应山古村·民居（一）

也叫彰应山村，这里的古民居一色的青砖黛瓦，青石条屋角和硬山屋顶，厅堂式二层结构，前有天窗天井，后有屏墙，左右厢房。

Yingshan Historic Village · Residence (1)

All of the historic civilian houses here share the same black-brick-black-tile two-storey style, with skylight windows, front patios, screen walls in back and living rooms at both sides.

应山古村·民居（二）

村内建筑多为单檐硬山顶，马头式山墙。屋宇建筑大多数为中轴结构，大门上的雨棚造型多种多样，并且雕龙画凤。

Yingshan Historic Village · Residence (2)

Most houses in the village use the middle axis structure with shields engraved with dragon or phoenix.

应山古村·飞檐

应山村古建筑，清一色的清水墙、青砖、灰瓦、木梁结构，青石条屋角、屋檐留有钩头滴水，两侧墙多保留风火墙。

Yingshan Historic Village • Flying Ridges

All the historic buildings in Yingshan have the black-brick-grey-tile style with wooden columns, with black stone strips in the corners, rain spouts in the ridges and fireproofing walls on the sidewalls.

| 应山石桥 |

　　古称玉环大石桥，建于清乾隆三十二年（1767年），位于乐昌应山古村南。石桥采用拱圈式纵联砌置法拱砌，南北走向，桥长49.85米，桥面宽6.5米。

Yingshan Stone Bridge
Built in 1767 south of Yingshan Old Village in Lechang, it is 49.85 meters long north-south and 6.5 meters wide.

户昌山村·全景

村子所处的地理位置优越，山环水绕，四周山岗重峦叠嶂，山中古树参天，山间泉水流淌；村中所建的房屋坐向不一致，有坐南向北的，有坐西朝东的，主体是坐西向东。人杰地灵，文化底蕴深厚

Huchangshan Village

The Hu Chang village is well located with mountains and waters surrounding. The houses are facing different directions, mostly east. It is a village with talented people and outstanding cultural heritage.

> 户昌山村·建筑

　　距今已有800多年历史，位于乐昌市庆云镇。建筑以村中央宗祠为中心，道路四通八达，村内保留着大量明清古建筑群。

Huchangshan Village · Buildings

The village in Qingyun, Lechang County, is more than 800 years old. In the center of the village is the ancestral temple with roads radiating in every direction. Many Ming and Qing Dynasty buildings are well preserved here.

户昌山村·灰塑

绝大部分房子有彩画，在每一家的大门上的横门梁都是雕龙刻凤，或是雕刻文官武将，或是飞禽走兽，至今图案还非常清晰。

Huchangshan Village • Plaster Engravings

Most of the houses have colored paintings of engraved dragon, phoenix, civil and military officers, flying birds, and beasts. The paintings can still be clearly seen.

甘棠镇村

始建于明万历年间（1573~1620年），位于乐昌黄圃。村内清一色的清代建筑，青砖灰瓦，木梁结构，建筑以中轴线布局为主体。

Gantangzhen Village
Built between 1573 and 1620 in Huangpu, Lechang, the houses are mostly Qing Dynasty style wooden structures of black bricks and grey tiles.

通济桥

俗称"大桥",建于清代,位于乳源县城。东西横跨杨溪水上游石高溪,东枕插天榜山,西纳铺街,清代大桥古八景之——桥亭文峰。

Tongji Bridge

Built during the Qing Dynasty in downtown Ruyuan County, the bridge crossed Shigao Stream, upstream of Yang Stream. To the east is Mount Chatianbang, to the west Pu Street.

[文昌塔]

建于明万历十二年（1584年），位于乳源鹰峰东路。葫芦塔刹，六角七层青砖石灰浆胶泥砌筑，高21.2米。高度逐层缩小，各层以菱角牙砖和平行间挑檐砖叠。

Wenchang Tower

Built in 1584 in Yingfeng EastRoad, Ruyuan, this seven-storey hexagonal tower had a gourd-shaped Tasha, 21 meters high; each storey had water chestnut-shaped brick ridges.

文塔

建于明代，位于乳源侯公渡镇。为平面为六角形空筒式砖木结构。葫芦刹塔顶以砖叠涩成顶。塔身室楼面开方孔作为楼门通达上下。

Wen Tower

Built during the Ming Dynasty in Hougongdu, Ruyuan County, the hexagonal brick and wood tower has gates to connect each floor.

云门寺

因其地处云门山下,所以俗称"云门寺"。建于后梁龙德三年(923年),位于乳源云门山,是禅宗"一花五叶"之一的云门宗开宗道场。寺内建有虚云纪念堂和舍利塔。

Yunmen Temple

Built in 923 at Yunmen Mountain, Ruyuan County, the temple includes Xuyun Memorial Hall and Sharia Pagoda.

云门寺·舍利塔

　　云门寺建在慈悲峰下,山高水长,修竹密林,环境清幽。此塔为舍利塔,常受信徒顶礼参拜。

Yunmen Temple · Sharia Pagoda

Yunmen Temple was built at the foot of Compassionate Peak, amid mountains and rivers, in a quiet forest setting. This pagoda is called Sharia Pagoda.

观澜书院（一）

建于清乾隆五十八年（1793）年，位于乳源大桥镇。为四进院落四合院式布局，砖木结构，悬山式顶的两层楼房。门楼筑有风火式山墙。

Guanlan Academy (1)
Built in 1793 in Daqiao, Ruyuan County, the four-entrance courtyard is made of brick and wood, with fireproofing walls at the gateways.

观澜书院（二）

书院一进为拱秀门、二进为观澜门、三进为明德堂、四进为资深堂。三个天井：一进天井地板镶铺鹅卵石，二、三井天井镶铺石板。

Guanlan Academy (2)

This four-entrance courtyard has three patios.

必背瑶寨（一）

必背瑶寨地处广东省韶关乳源瑶族自治县城东北54千米的崇山峻岭中，因有小山形如鳖鱼背，故名"鳖背"，由于"鳖"字笔画多难写，以谐音"必"字代之，改为"必背"。

Bibei Yao Village (1)

Located in the deep mountains north-east of Ruruan Autonomous County of Shaoguan in Guangdong Province, the mountain, shaped like the back of the turtle, thus the name Biebei in Chinese. Bie in Chinese is the sophisticated written form, later it was replaced by the common formBi, thus the name Bibei.

必背瑶寨（二）

房屋多为杉皮、杉木建造，也有的是土砖青瓦建筑。有的村寨是多间平列，也有的是"上居下牧"的双层屋结构。

Bibei Yao Village (2)

Located in Dayao Mountain, Ruyuan County, the buildings are made mostly of Chinese fir. In some villages people live upstairs and livestock downstairs.

> 八角塔

建于清康熙四十年（1701年），位于翁源县坝仔镇，共五层八角，高26.7米，除首层用沙质石砌结外，其余各层均用青砖砌结。

Bajiao Tower

Built in 1701 in Bazai, Wengyuan County, this five-storey octagonal brick tower is 26.7 meters tall.

翁源八卦围（一）

这座罕见大围的房屋构造及规划完全按八卦样式设计建造。建筑群以祠堂为中心，左右和中后房屋按八卦层层加串，向外伸延，共有1653间房，99条街巷。

Eight-Diagram Shaped Building in Wengyuan (1)

This rare enclosed house was designed in the shape of the ancient eight diagrams, with the ancestral temple in the middle, extending in eight directions as the eight diagrams. It has 1653 rooms and 99 corridors.

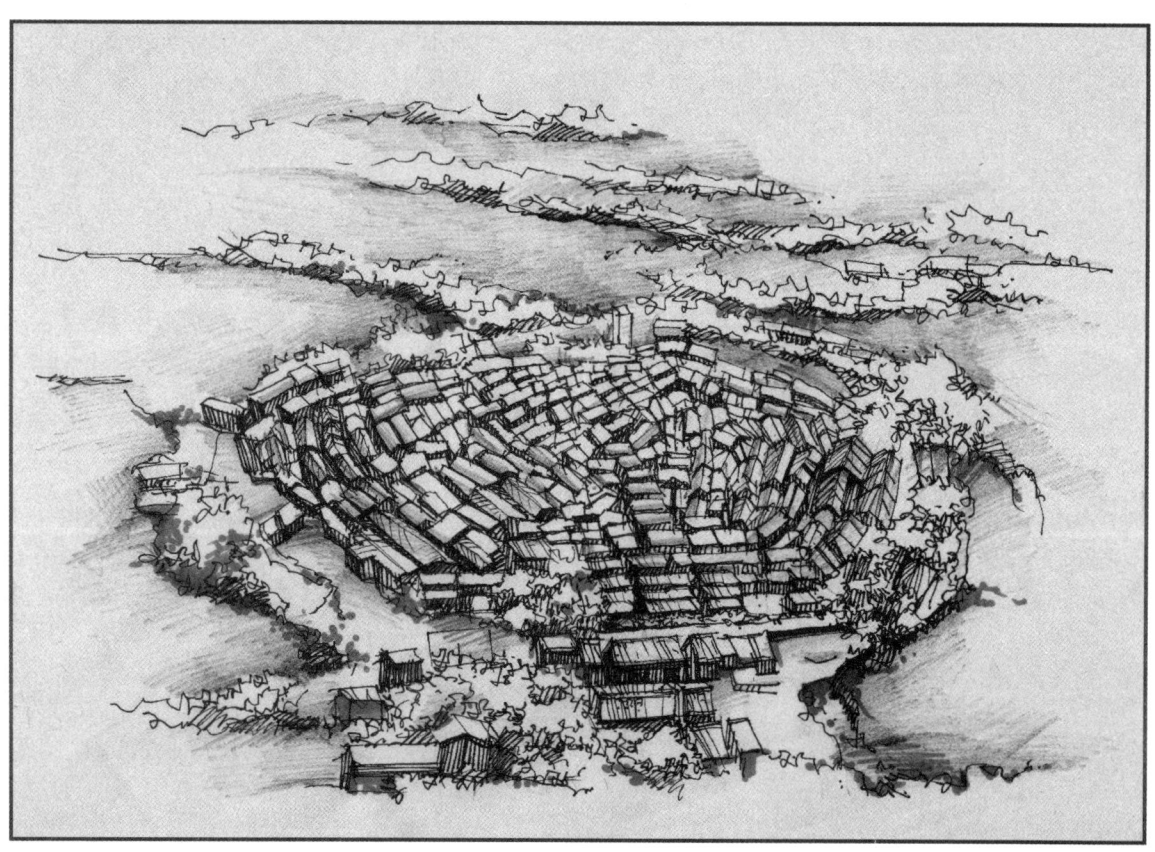

翁源八卦围（二）

围内房屋从外至内由高到低排列，屋形非常怪异，有的像一段弧线，有的微呈梯形，还有的仿似镰刀，几乎没有一间是方形。

Eight-Diagram shaped Building in Wengyuan (2)

The rooms are arranged from outside to inside, from high land to low land, with very unusual shapes; like arcs, ladders or sickles, but no square rooms.

湖心坝客家群楼

建于明正统间（1436~1449年），位于江尾镇南塘村。占地150公顷，59座围楼形成楼外有楼、楼中有楼。群楼小巷连大街，纵横有序，红麻石砌井，鹅卵石铺巷。

Hakka Building Complex, Huxinba

Built between 1436 and 1449 in Nantang, Weijiang, the complex had 59 buildings with connecting alleys.

湖心坝客家群楼（二）

围楼楼外有楼、楼中有楼，在茫茫田野上构成一幅立体的《清明上河图》。如此庞大的客家民居建筑群，可亦称粤北客家第一村。

Hakka Building Complex, Huxinba (2)

The buildings outside and inside comprise a vivid three-dimensional picture of Riverside Scene of Qingming Festival in the vast space. With such great Hakka private building complex, it can be called Number One Hakka Village in North Guangdong.

湖心坝客家群楼（三）

楼群中有造型各异的古围楼、雕龙画凤的墙扇屏风、清静幽雅的民居小屋。民风纯朴，民居典雅，古街古巷，古井古桥。

Hakka Building Complex, Huxinba (3)

There are types of old enclosed houses with carved dragon and painted phoenix on the screens and walls. All the old streets, alleys, wells and bridges, create a quiet and picturesque scene.

葱茅围

俗称"八卦围""老围子""太围子",始建于元至正二十七年(1367年),位于翁源县。外墙基座及墙角转折处用细红砂岩方条石,上砌大鹅卵石墙,密布瞭望孔、射击孔。

Simaowei

Built in 1367 in Wenyuan County, the outside wall base and corners are made of blocks of fine red sandstone, with cobblestone main walls densely dotted with observation and shooting apertures.

古民居石雕

村内至今保存有大量清代的盆座石、石墩、石水盆等木雕和石雕，精美绝伦。

Stone Engraving of Historic House Relics

Many Qing Dynasty wood and stone engravings such as standing stones, and seat stones and stone basins are well preserved in the village.

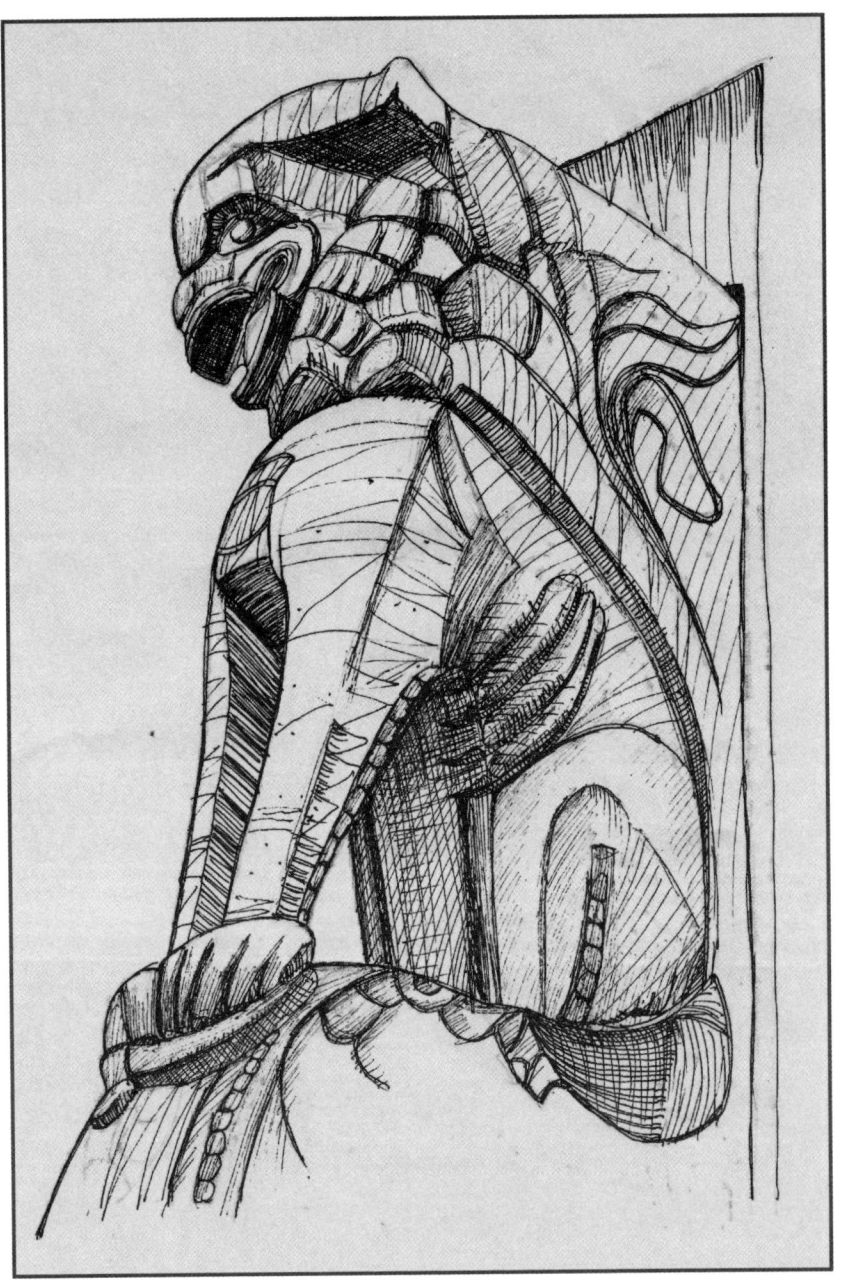

韶关市·仁化县、始兴县、新丰县
Shaoguan City · Renhua County, Shixing County, Xinfeng City

> 普同塔

建于清顺治五年（1648年），位于仁化县。为平面八角三层楼阁式石塔，高3.6米，红砂石砖砌筑。首层正对香炉设拱券形龛，各层檐角上翘。

Putong Tower

Built in 1648 in Renhua County, the three-storey, octagonal red granite tower is 3.6 meters tall.

东庄门楼

建于清乾隆年间（1736～1795年），位于仁化黄坑镇。大门楼为砖木结构，重檐歇山顶；小门楼为红砂岩条石结构，檐下设石雕斗拱。

Dongzhuang Gateway

Built between 1736 and 1795, the gateway is in Huangkeng, Renhua County. The major gateway was built of brick and wood, the smaller of red granite.

云龙寺塔

原名西山寺塔，建于唐乾宁年间（894~898年），位于仁化县董塘镇。为平面四方形四角五级仿楼阁式砖塔，高10.34米。用仿木构筑法，砖砌出倚柱、栏额等。

Yunlong Temple Pagoda

Built between 894 and 898, in Dongtang, Renhua County, the square, five-storey pagoda is 10 meters tall.

石塘村

位于仁化县西南面石塘镇盆地中，建于明清时期，已有600多年历史。村庄周围山清水秀，环境幽静，村子历史悠久，文化深厚，人杰地灵，诞生多位历史名人。石塘村共有古建筑133座，保存完好的有106座。

Shitang Village

Located in the basin of Shitang town, southwest of Renhua County, it has a history of more than six hundred years. The beautiful mountains and waters features in the old village and the quiet surroundings and rich cultures make it a prosperous place. There are 133 old buildings in the village, among which 106 are well preserved.

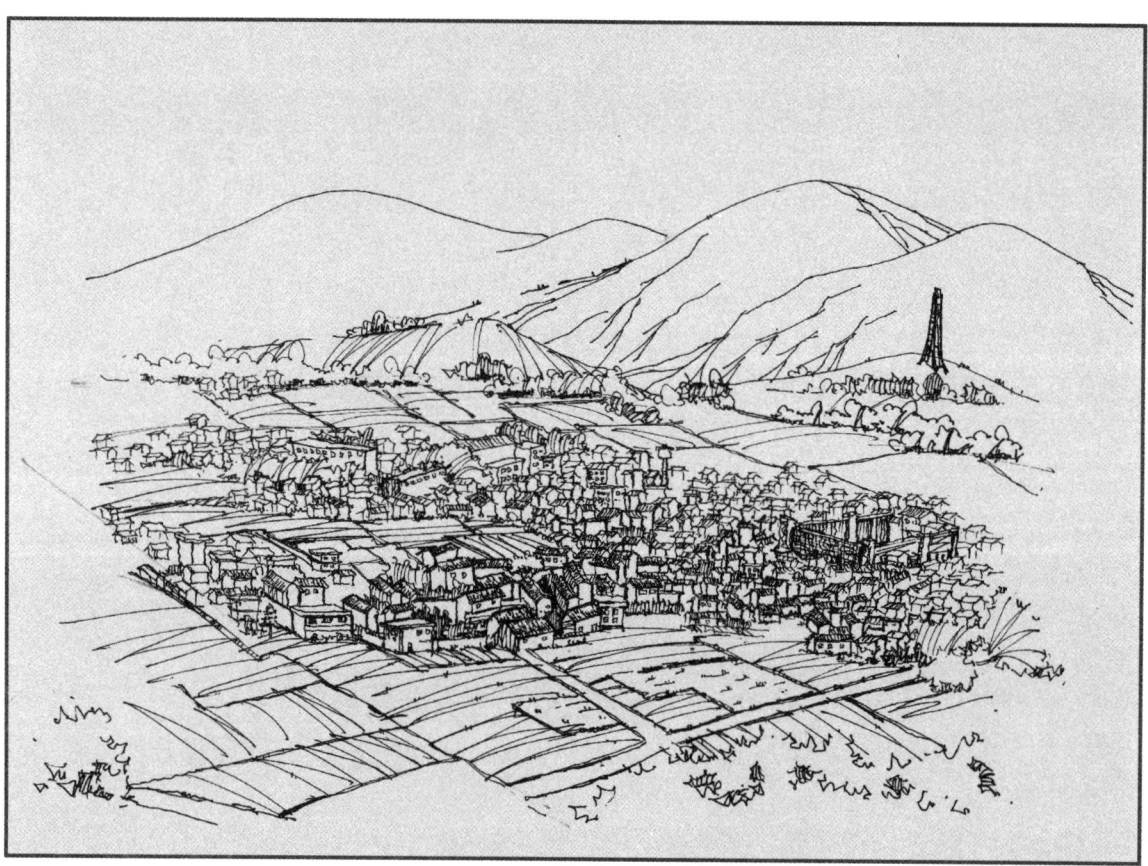

[石塘村·民居（一）]

村中房屋存在多种建筑风格并存的现象，在建筑形制和建造技术上体现地方典型性（客家夯土建筑），还受江西（青砖）建筑风格的影响。

Shitang Village • Civilian Residence (1)

The Hakka rammed earth buildings are greatly influenced by the brick style of Jiangxi architecture.

> 石塘村·民居（二）

民居属于徽派建筑，由上等青砖青瓦砌成，高墙飞檐，堂皇美观。精致的青砖、封火山墙则颇有徽派建筑的韵味。

Shitang Village • Civilian Residence (2)

This Anhui Style civilian residence built of first quality black brick and tiles, features high walls and flying eaves. The delicate black bricks and Anhui style fire gable create a splendid scene.

石塘村民居·古巷

石塘古村的巷到大都用鹅卵石铺成，纵横交错，错综复杂，条条街巷均有闸门，就像进入迷宫，极易迷路。

Civilian Residence in Shitang Village • Old Alleys

The crisscrossing alleys in Shitang village are mostly paved with cobblestones. There are gates in every alley; just like a maze, it is easy to get lost here.

石塘村民居·高墙

两边是马头墙，橡牙翘角，高出瓦面，既美观又防火。

Civilian Residence in Shitang Village • High Walls

These fire-resistant houses, with horsehead walls at both sides, are topped with stretching eaves above the tile, giving a sensational view.

石塘村民居·大门

呈正方形,正房、厢房错落有致,院落房房相同。院落里面的每个房间、厅堂、天井,都与走廊、巷道、楼梯相连通,大门设置在屋的左侧。

Civilian Residence in Shitang Village • Front Door

The squared front door is usually situated on the left of the house, with the main living rooms and wing rooms lining the courtyard. The rooms, halls, and patios all connect viacorridors, alleys and stairs.

石塘村·祠堂（一）

历史村内上共有九座祠堂，现存：三多堂、礼园祠堂、奉先堂、妥侑堂、贻德堂、蔡屋祠堂、高祠堂等七座，六座为李氏祠堂，一座为蔡氏祠堂。

Shitang Village · Ancestral Temple (1)

There are nine ancestral temples in the village, six belonging to the Li family and one to the Cai family.

[石塘村·祠堂（二）]

17世"熙春公"所建的"贻德祠堂"是村中现存规模最大、保存最完好的一座祠堂。

Shitang Village · Ancestral Temple (2)

This temple is the largest and the most well-preserved in Shitang.

石塘村·祠堂（三）

村内祠堂均属于徽派建筑，厅前有天井，天井前面有照壁，厅的两侧是房间，房间少，窗户小，房内冬暖夏凉。

Shitang Village · Ancestral Temple (3)

This Hui style architecture has a patio in front of the hall and a screen wall in front of the patio. On both sides of the hall are small rooms with small windows. The rooms are warm in winter and cool in summer.

双峰寨

始建于清光绪二十五年（1899年），位于仁化县石塘镇。巨型寨堡，外形成长方形，石灰及青砖砌成。外围由护城河、吊桥和两重寨门组成，平面呈"回"字形，中间是一大片草坪。

Shuangfeng Village

Built in 1899 in Shitang, Renhua County, it is a huge rectangle stockade village built with lime and black bricks. It is protected by a river, suspension bridge and double village gates.

双峰寨·侧面

　　古城堡攻、防、守环环紧扣，以一个主楼（也称中楼）和四个炮楼为主轴，东西两面城墙中间各有个瞭望台，其间用围墙相连。

Shuangfeng Zhai • Side

This old castle combined offense and defense, one reinforcing the other. The main Central Tower, together with the four gun turrets is the castle axis. On eastern and western sides of the wall, two observation towers connect the perimeter fortifications.

双峰寨·内部

　　大革命时期被中共广东省委誉为"继海陆丰农民运动"后农民暴动中最伟大的战斗——双峰寨保卫战就发生在这里。

Shuangfeng Stockade • Interior Scene

During the Great Revolution Period (1927-1928), the Shuangfeng Defensive Battle took place here; so, the Stockade of Shuangfeng was granted the title National Relic Protection Unit.

{丹霞山（一）}

又称中国红石公园，号称"露天的地质博物馆"或"天然的性文化博物馆"，位于韶关市仁化县，面积达290平方千米。

Mount Danxia (1)

Also named Red Stone Park in China and Natural Geological Museum, the park, located in Renhua County, Shaoguan City, has an area of 290 km².

> 丹霞山（二）

形成于距今1.4亿年至7000万年间，是世界丹霞地貌中发育最典型、类型最齐全、造型最丰富的景色。

Mount Danxia (2)

Formed 140~70 million years ago, Mount Danxia is a typical landform of red terrestrial sandstone with the most diversified features.

周所塔

建于明代，位于始兴城南镇。六角七层木板楼阁式叠檐砖塔，无顶。每层以砖叠出双檐，抹角柱，内各层均有拱角柱、阑额和斗拱。

Zhousuo Tower

Built during the Ming Dynasty in Chengnan, Shixing County, the seven-storey hexagonal roofless brick tower has folded eaves.

广州会馆

建于清咸丰八年（1858年），位于始兴县。正屋分前中后三栋，每栋瓦面两翼筑风火墙相连，以绿色琉璃瓦盖面，前后两端翘起。

Guangzhou Hall

Built in 1858, this Hall in Shixing County is composed of three buildings, front, middle and back, each connected by fireproofing walls covered with green glazed tiles.

满堂客家大围

位于始兴县，尚保存有200座左右。隘子镇的满堂大围是最具代表性的，建于清道光十六年（1836年），由当时的富豪官乾荣所建，占地一万多平方米。

Mantang Hakka Manor

Mantang Hakka Manor in Shixing County is among more than two hundred well preserved houses. The manor in Aizi Town is the most representative. With an area of more than ten thousand square meters. It was built in 1836 by a wealthy man named Guan Qianrong,.

满堂客家大围·民居（一）

建于清道光十六年（1836年），位于始兴县隘子镇。由上、中、下三个小围楼连接构成，中围楼主墙基全部用河卵石砌成，墙体上布满了各种瞭望孔、射击孔。

Hakka Walled Houses • Residence (1)

Built in 1836 in Aizi, Shixing County, the house has three smaller, connected walled houses, with observation and shooting apertures in the walls.

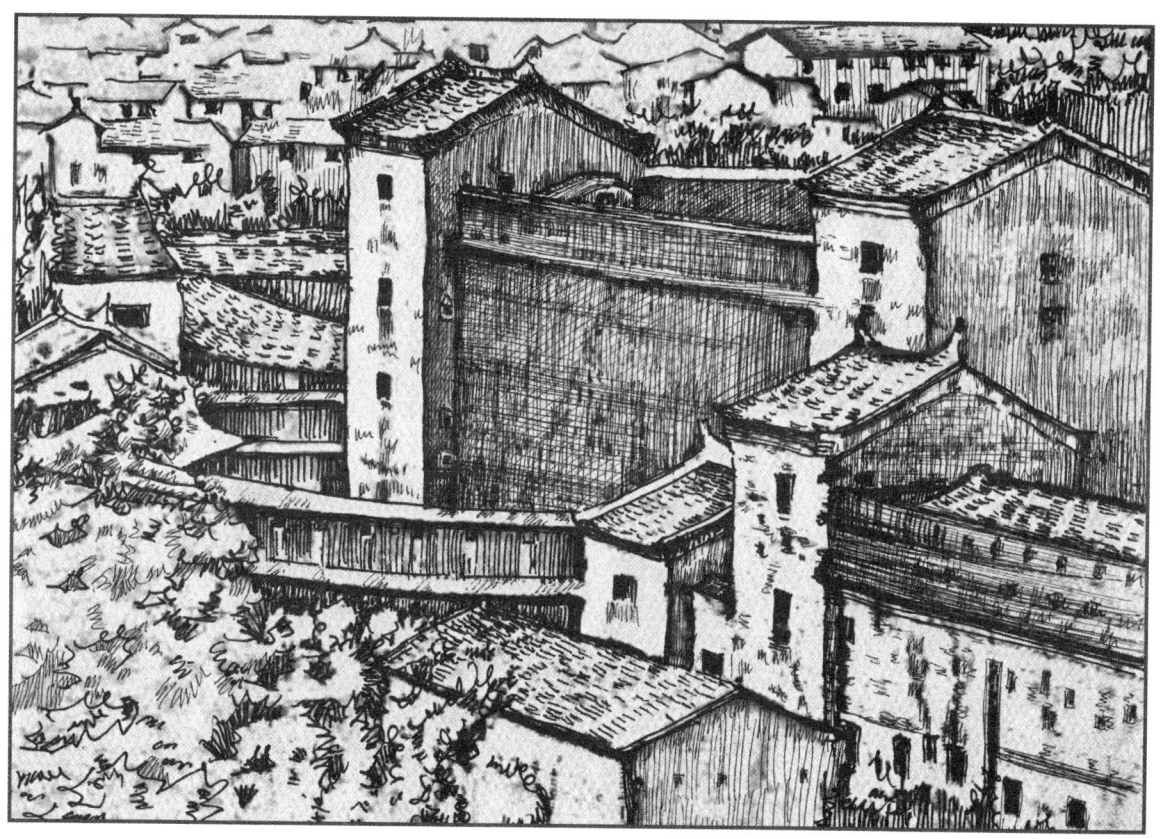

满堂客家大围·民居（二）

围楼是客家民居最有特色的建筑之一，属砖石结构，非常坚固，其建筑布局是北方古代城堡和四合院住宅的结合。

Hakka Walled Houses • Residence (2)

The walled house is a major feature of Hakka dwellings. Built solidly of brick and stone, they blend the structure of the old castles in the north and quadrangle courtyard.

| 满堂客家大围·内部 |

在建筑风格上,既有古代的雄浑朴实的气势,又有近代精致高雅的韵味。集古代、近代客家建筑风格为一体,具有较高的科学和艺术价值

Mantang Hakka Manor · Interior Scene

It blends the splendor of ancient styles and the delicacy of modern styles, of high scientific and aesthetic value.

满堂客家大围·天井

围楼内有天井16个、水井四口，用人工磨制过青砖铺砌而成，显得光滑规整。门框、窗框、台阶、廊沿、井台等以花岗岩石条砌成，显得坚实大方。

Hakka Walled House · Patio

There are 16 patios and 4 wells within this walled house. The gate frames and window frames, stairs, corridors and wells are all built of granite.

满堂客家大围·灰塑

古称灰批，材料以石灰为主，作品依附于建筑墙壁上沿和屋脊上或其他建筑工艺上，是岭南传统建筑装饰工艺。

Hakka Walled House · Plaster Engravings

Also called grey lime, this is a traditional decoration craft in Lingnan.

| 东湖坪村·祠堂 |

　　始建于清代,有建筑九栋十八厅、曾氏祠堂、永成堂围楼、藏宝秘图与曾氏银库等。建筑结构独特,建造坚固,雄浑古朴,反映着当年客家文化的丰硕和经济富庶。

Donghuping Village • Ancestral Temple
Built during the Qing Dynasty (1644-1911), it is comprised of 9 buildings totaling 18 rooms. The structure is unique and solid, reflecting the cultural and economic influence of Hakka at that time.

东湖坪民俗文化村

始建于清代,建筑结构独特,建造坚固,雄浑古朴,反映着当年客家文化的丰硕和经济富庶。

Donghuping Folk Culture Village

First built during the Qing Dynasty, the structures are unique and very sturdy, reflecting the richness of the Hakka culture and economy.

东湖坪民俗文化村·牌坊

由三座牌坊组成,为四柱三开间的门楼式牌坊,竖立在要道之上。

Donghuping Folk Culture Village · Memorial Gateway
It has three gateways, each with four columns and three gates.

东湖坪民俗文化村·永成堂围楼

建于清光绪二十一年（1895年），整栋建筑物砖、石、木结构，长方形，四角为炮楼，是碉堡与民宅的结合形式，四层楼都有统一的回廊过道，上下四通八达。

Donghuping Folk Culture Village · Yongchengtang Walled House

Built in 1895, the rectangle walled house is a combination of castle and civilian house with the four corners serving as the gun turrets. Corridors connecting each floor makes it convenient to go up and down.

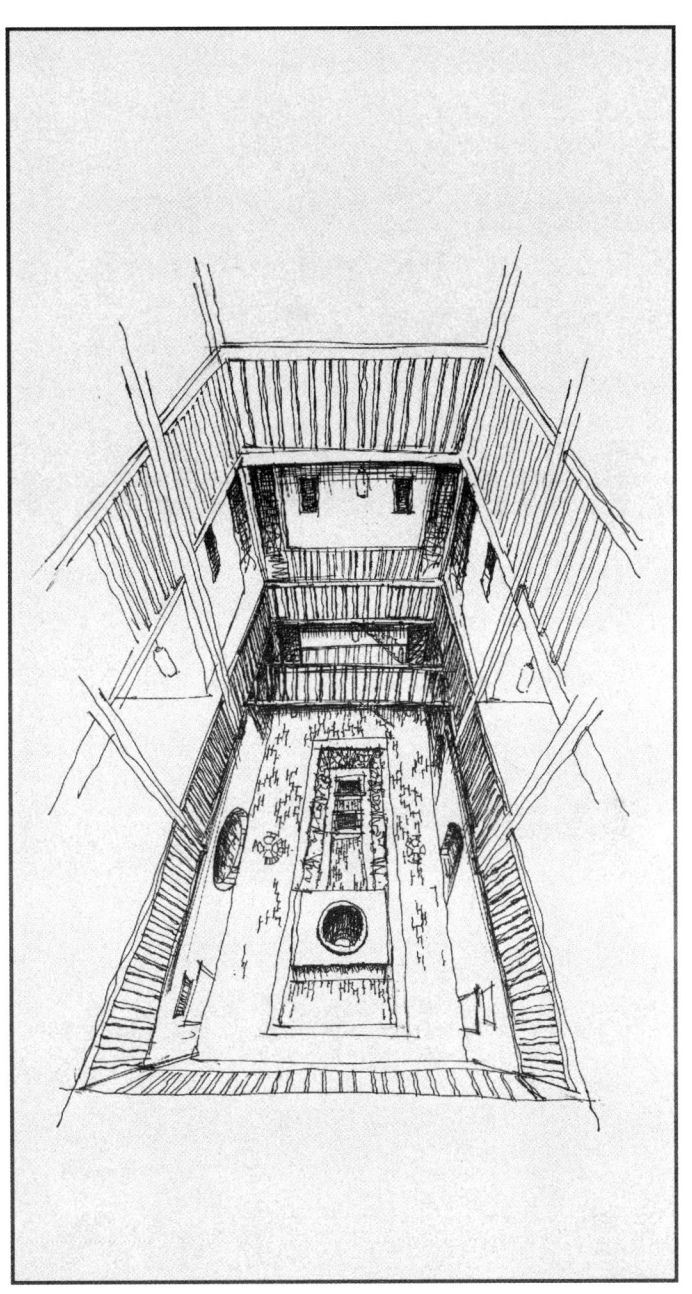

东湖坪民俗文化村·灰塑

在青砖上雕出花卉、人物等图案,是古建筑雕刻中很重要的一种艺术形式。主要用来装饰寺、庙、观、庵及民居的构件和墙面。

Donghuping Folk Culture Village • Plaster Engraving

Flowers and human images were engraved on the black bricks. This was the most important art form in historic architectural engravings.

九栋十八井（一）

建于清康熙五十三年（1714年），位于新丰县。为三进院落四合院式布局，整体平面基本上是椭圆形，屋前为禾坪，再往前是池塘，屋后是的山坡、林地。

Nine-Buildings-Eighteen-Patios (1)

Built in 1714 in Xinfeng County, the three-entrance quadrangle courtyard was oval-shaped, with threshing ground and pond in front.

九栋十八井（二）

墙体楼阁均使用火砖到顶。屋心房间部分采用卵石用石灰沙浆砌筑，亦有部分用泥砖砌墙。天井内檐阶用长石条嵌镶。

Nine-Buildings-Eighteen-Patios (2)

Outside walls were built of fired-clay bricks while rooms within used cobblestone and lime; patios were decorated with long stone strips.

清远市·连州市、英德市、佛冈县、清新县
Qingyuan City · Lianzhou City, Yingde City, Fogang City, Qinxin County

丰阳古村（一）

距今已有1000多年的历史，位于连州市。现还遗存着丰富的宋代人文景观和完好的明清建筑。连州市是广东古村落保存得最为完整的地方之一。

Fengyang Historic Village (1)

This 1,000 year-year-old village, with many cultural landscapes of Song Dynasty and well-preserved Ming and Qing architecture is one of many well-preserved old villages in Guangdong.

丰阳古村（二）

一幢家庙、两条古街、三间祠堂、四座门楼，这些古老的建筑包容了丰阳古村的全部内涵。

Yangfeng Historic Village (2)

A clan temple, two historic streets, three ancestral temples and four gateways comprise old Fengyang Village.

> 白鹤寨

山奇峰突兀,山色秀丽。村中明清时期的建筑居多,最有特色是一幢清代的四合院式的老屋。

Baihe Village

The village provides a very beautiful view of the spectacular sharp peaked mountains. Most of the buildings are from the Ming and Qing Dynasties; the most featured is an old Qing quadrangle courtyard.

> 白家城

　　始建于清康熙五十三年（1467年），位于连州市东陂镇，是连州古村落里面积最小、保存最好、最具建筑特色和民俗特色的古村落。为广东省第三批古村落保护对象。

Baijiacheng Village

Built in 1467 in Dongpo Town, Lianzhou City, of all the old villages in Lianzhou, Baijiacheng is the smallest, yet has the best preserved special architecture.

| 慧光塔 |

始建于 468 年，位于连州市慧光公园内。塔高 50 米，九层十七级，每层用砖砌出角柱，层层向上递减，呈直线收缩，造型美观，是省重点保护文物。

Huiguang Tower

Built in 468 in Huiguang Park in Lianzhou City, the 50 meters Hightower and has nine stories and seventeen stairs. Every storey has brick corner columns, their number decreasing from the bottom to the top.

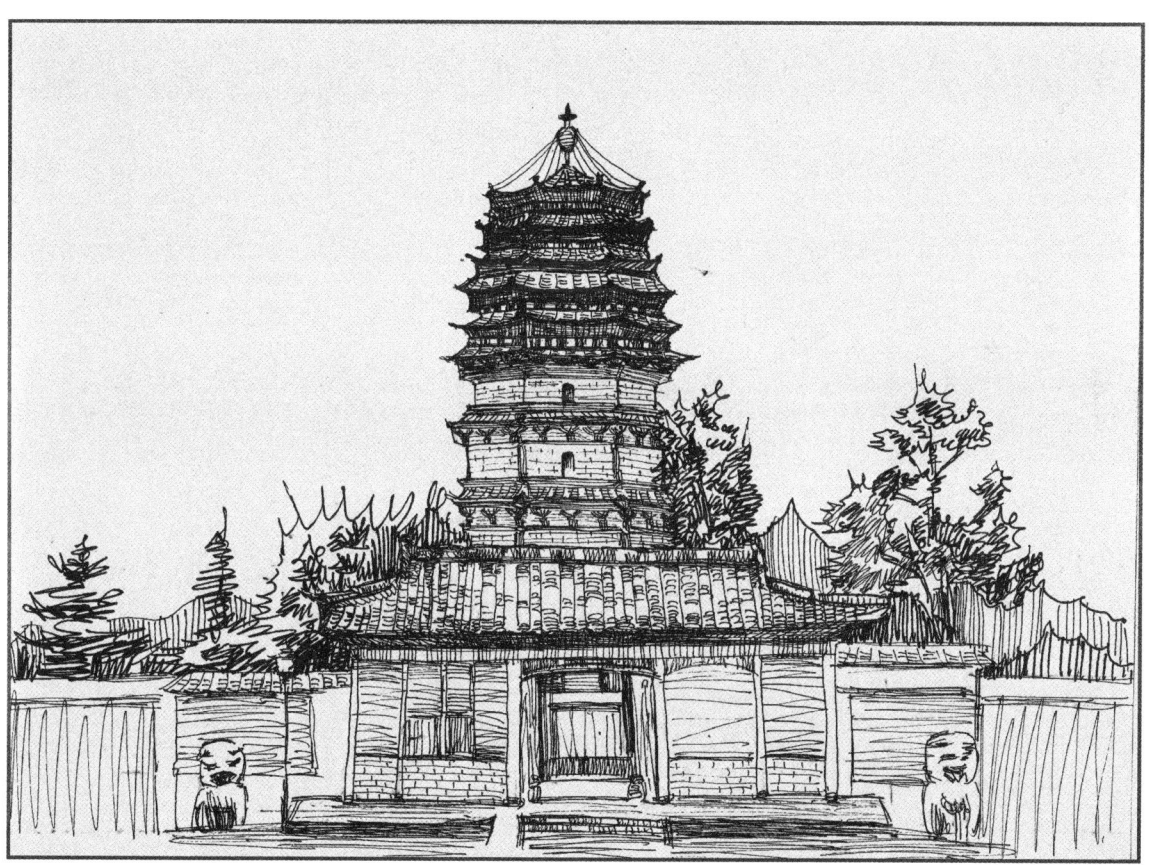

洪秀全传教屋

位于连州连南县的千年瑶寨。山寨建在易守难攻的半山腰,壁垒森严,寨门高约七米,宽约二米,门两边和顶上全是用坚硬的大石头垒成,寨门两侧用石头砌起一米厚围墙。

Missionary House, Hong Xiuquan

Located in this thousand-year-old Yao village in Liannan County of Lianzou City. The strongly fortified village was built on the mountain slope so as to prevent surprise attack. The village gateway between thick stone walls is 7 meters high and 2 meters wide.

丰溪古庙

建于北宋，为二进四合院式布局，典型的宋代建筑，古庙前的千年古榕和古戏台古韵盎然，四座门楼分别位于东南西北四个方位。

Fengxi Old Temple

Built during the Northern Song Dynasty (960~1127), the double-entrance courtyard is typical Song architecture. A thousand-year-old banyan tree and an old theater stage are in the front.

> 卿罡古村

村内民居建筑群、城墙、门楼、祠堂，基本保留完整。古井水质特别清澈，围绕着这口井的青石板路延伸至全村的每个角落。

Qinzhen Old Village

The houses, city walls, gateways and ancestral temples are well preserved. Black stone paths around the clear-water well extend to every corner of the village.

彭家祠（一）

位于英德市西南部的螺山，彭家祠为当地彭姓人家的祖祠堂，座南朝北，整个建筑封闭，自成一体。房屋从山脚至山顶共分三层，山高约33米。

Peng Clan Academy (1)

On Luo Mountain in southwestern Yingde City, the Peng Clan Academy was the Peng Clan ancestral temple. The three-storey, 33m-high, building sits on the south, facing north.

彭家祠（二）

此建筑为抵御土匪滋扰而建的防御型堡垒，从山脚到山顶只有一条石阶通道，360 级。乡间称之为"寨山古堡"，1995 年 12 月被列为县级文物保护单位。

Peng Clan Academy (2)
Built to defend local bandit attacks, there is only one stone stair path with 360 steps from the foot to the top of the mountain. Locally it is called Old Castle. In December, 1995 it was listed as a county level Relics Preservation Unit.

蓬莱寺塔

建于唐咸通年间（860~874年），位于洽洸镇东北。因塔砖有"舍利弗"阳文，又称"舍利塔"。塔高15.4米，为平面六角五层楼阁式砖室塔。宋代曾重修。

Penglai Temple Pagoda
Built between 860-874, and rebuilt during the Song Dynasty, northeast of Hanguang Town, the five-storey hexagonal brick pagoda is 15.4 meters high.

老地湾

　　距今已有300余年的历史，位于英德北江河畔。老地湾背山临江，村后左峰为海螺山，呈半月形翠屏，将整个村落紧拥入怀，"老地湾"由此得名。

Laodi Bay

Embraced by Hailuo Mountain facing North River in Yingde, the 300+ year-old village is named Laodi Bay.

> 林公祠

建于清道光二十一年（1841年），位于英德老地湾。为三进二天池格式布局。祠堂和民居有侧门相通，间天井为麻石所凿成，雨水从天井的暗道排出，是清代标准的民间建筑。

Lin Clan Ancestral Temple

Built in 1841, in Laodi Bay, Yingde City, the three-entrance-two-tianchi style is Qing architecture. Side doors are common in ancestral temples and civilian houses.

【赵氏宗祠】

位于英德市区南。老地湾有三个祠堂,清代民间建筑。基本呈水平分布,朝选林公祠居中,左为黄氏私塾,右是赵氏宗祠,再右为林氏家族住宅。

Zhao Clan Academy

Located south of Yingde City, three ancestral academies were built in Laodi Bay during the Qing Dynasty. Lin Clan academy is in the middle, with Huang clan academy and Zhao clan academy to the left and right respectively. Right of Zhao Clan academy are the Lin clan homes.

上岳古村（一）

　　始建于南宋，位于佛冈县龙山镇。整个村庄依山而建，环水而设，全村分为十八里，十八口鱼塘分布在村中各里。

Shangyue Historic Village (1)

Built during Southern Song Dynasty (1127~1279) in Longshan Town of Fogang County, the village was built against the mountains the facing water, with eighteen fishponds altogether.

上岳古村（二）

村内房屋清一色青砖黛瓦，雕梁画栋，"锅耳楼"高低错落，气势恢宏。古物古迹、灰塑彩绘、浮雕木刻随处可见，栩栩如生，具有鲜明的岭南建筑艺术风格。

Shangyue Historic Village (2)

All of the buildings in the village feature typical Lingnan architectural style with black bricks, glazed tiles, wood engravings on the columns, plaster engravings and basso-relievo.

上岳古村（三）

上岳古民居是目前广东规模较大、保存较完好的古村落，具有重要的历史文化价值和建筑风貌特色。现为广东省第七批省级文物保护单位。

Shangyue Historic Village (3)

Civilian houses here are the largest of the well-preserved relics with most significant historic and cultural architectural value. It is the seventh group of Guangdong Provincial Relics Protection Unit.

> 上岳古村（四）

　　锅耳墙又称为"鳌头墙"，有"独占鳌头"的寓意。上岳古村随处可见高低错落的锅耳墙。

Shangyue Historic Village (4)

The Pan ear-shaped wall is also called Aotou wall, which means "on the top". This type of wall is seen everywhere in Shangyue village.

| 乾隆皇家大院 |

　　坐落于清新县河洞乡。建于清乾隆二十三年（1758年），村子坐南朝北，规划整齐有九巷十八进直说，是粤北地区保存着最好最完整的清代年间的房屋建筑群之一。

Empire Courtyard of Qianlong

This well-preserved Qing building complex in the northern Guangdong region was built in 1758 in Hedong Town, Qingxin County. The well-designed village with 9 alleys and 18 entrances is seated on the south, facing north.

> 七星岗塔

建于 1921 年，塔为八角五层仿楼阁式建筑，青砖砌墙，面朝东北，高近 20 米，平面呈正八边形，属于风水塔。

Qixinggang Tower
Built in 1921, the five-storey octagonal black brick pavilion-like tower is about 20 meters tall. It has geomantic omen significance.

> 清远楼

又名钟楼,始建于明成化十八年(1482年),全楼高25米,是一座重檐多角十字脊歇山顶的高大建筑。为我国古代建筑的精品,现为全国重点文物保护单位。

Qingyuan Building

Built in 1482 at a height of 25 meters, it is a splendid ancient architectural multi-eave, multi-cornice building with cross ridges and gable-hip roof.

故乡里民俗文化主题公园

建于2005年，位于清新县王子山脉脚下，有"岭南民间故宫"之称。建筑直接选取来自岭南水乡古镇的古旧材料，并采用原址搬迁的建筑方式，以传统的手工艺建造而成。

Guxiangli Folk Culture Theme Park

Built in 2005, at the foot of Wangzi mountain ridge in Qingxin County, nicknamed the Local Imperial Palace of Liangnan, it is made of hand crafted building materials from old villages in Liangnan.

民风民俗
Folk Customs

瑶族·刺绣

瑶族"好五色衣裳",是对先祖纪念的一种标志。刺绣的用途主要是配饰在服饰上,花纹颜色有红、绿、黄、黑、白五种。

Yao Minority · Embroidery

The fine five-color clothes of the Yao minority commemorate their ancestors. The five embroidery colors are: red, green, yellow, black, white.

瑶族·反面刺绣

从反面绣，绣时不用画底稿，先用黑白线依布纹绣出方格，然后于各格中配入基本图案；常用意象化、象形化的图案构成主要内容。

Yao Minority • "Opposing" Embroidery

Embroidering starts from the opposite side without drawing the picture beforehand. Squares are first embroidered using black and white thread following the woven marks then, basic designs are filled in.

瑶族·小长鼓舞

长鼓舞是瑶族民间歌舞的典型代表。长鼓约四尺长,两头大,中间小,呈喇叭形。舞时横挂在腰间,右手五指并拢,以掌拍鼓。

Yao Minority • Little Long Drum Dance

The long drum is about 4 chi long with the ends bigger than the middle. Dancers attach it to the waist and strike it with their palms.

瑶族·长鼓舞

又称黄鼓舞,长鼓中的一种,分公鼓、母鼓两种。跳舞时以母鼓为轴心,公鼓围绕母鼓跳转,并边舞边击鼓,动作变化多端。

Yao Minority • Long Drum Dance

Also called Yellow Drum Dance, using a type of long drum, it has male and female drummers. The female drummer dances in the center and the male drummers dance around.

> 瑶族·耍歌堂

耍歌堂是连南排瑶祭祀祖先，喜庆丰收的传统节庆，在明洪武年间（1368～1398年）已具规模，经过几百年的承传和发展。耍歌堂成为排瑶历史变迁、民间信仰、文化艺术、风情习俗的浓缩和集中表现。

Yao Minority · Shuage tang Festival

Shuagetang, which means celebrating the harvest in Yao language, is a traditional festival to worship ancestors and celebrate the harvest with a history of more than 600 years. Now it is a concentrated expression reflecting Pai Yao' history and folk.

瑶族·舞蹈

起舞时,舞者身穿节日盛装,腰扎红绸,脚裹白色绑腿。瑶族民间舞蹈是从瑶族民俗宗教祭祀活动演变而来,是民族文化的再现。

Yao Minority • Dance

Dancers dress in festive clothes with red silk cloth tied at the waist and white leggings. Yao cultural folk dance was evolved from their religious activities.

> 南华诞

又称"六祖诞"庙会,始于唐开元二年(714年),是宝林寺(后改名法泉寺)住持令韬为弘扬六祖禅法,保护六祖惠能真身,每年行的祭祀禅宗六祖的庙会活动。

Nanhua Birthday Celebration
Begun in 714 by Lingtao, Abbot of Baolin Temple (later Faquan Temple), the commemoration for the Sixth Patriarch is still practiced today.

采茶戏

约在清乾隆年间（1736～1795年）传入南雄。音乐唱腔由赣南采茶灯及南雄民间音乐组成。在表演艺术上运用打扇花，舞台表演应用矮步步法。

Tealeaf Picking Opera

Spreading to Nanxiong between 1736 and 1795, its singing style combines Tealeaf Picking opera in south Jiangxi and local folk music.

石塘月姐歌

每年农历八月初一"开坛"至八月十五"收坛",每天晚上妇女们就聚集在"月姐歌堂"里,内容包含了叙事歌、农事季节歌、情歌等。

Yuejie Song in Shitang

Every year from August 1 to 15 on the lunar calendar, women gather in Yuejie Theater at night to sing.

高桥舞狮

是中国优秀的传统民间艺术，每逢佳节或隆重庆典，民间都以狮舞来助兴，其特点是站在高跷上舞狮。

Lion Dance in Gaoqiao

This traditional folk art, characterized by walking on stilts and dancing, held on every festival, is how the folk entertain themselves.

双龙舞双狮

起源于清光绪三年（1877年），是南雄珠玑巷独特的民间艺术形式，表演者全用高步队形，音乐以打击乐伴奏为主。

Bi-dragon and Bi-lion Dance

Originated in 1877, in this unique folk art in Zhuji Alley, Nanxiong, performers walk on stilts with the accompaniment of drums.

十点梅花

始于唐代，是曲江农村舞狮系列锣鼓之中最优美动听的民间击乐精品，既可作舞狮的锣鼓，又可作单独表演。现在，逢年过节、庆丰收、婚礼、祝寿等在农村中均有表演，深受群众欢迎。

Shidian Meihua

Originated during the Tang Dynasty (618-907) this is the best folk music in Qujiang for the lion dance. It is popularly performed during festivals, harvests, weddings and anniversaries in the countryside.

舞纸马

原为一种祭祀舞蹈，新丰纸马从翁源礤下镇传入，当时只用于庆贺农村喜事，舞纸马可以分为单马、双马和群马。表演以马童、新郎、新娘、村姑为主。

Paper Horse Dance

Originally a sacrificial dance, this dance in Xinfeng was introduced from Caixia Town in Wengyuan. At that time it was only used to celebrate the happy events in the countryside. Paper Horse dance can be divided into single, double and group horse dance.

舞春牛

　　一般在腊月开始，用竹篾、棕绳、黑布、纸等扎成春牛。正月初一，春牛队出游村坊拜年，唱"十二月花"，叙述十二个月的农事生产知识。

Spring Bull Dance

Spring bulls are made of bamboo skin, coir rope, black cloth and paper. On 1st January, lunar calendar, a team of spring "bulls" parade along the village streets wishing everyone Happy New Year and singing "Twelve Flowers of the Months", depicting a knowledge of agricultural activities during the year.

乐昌三溪青蛙狮

俗称"蟾蜍狮",又名"神狮子"。由六至九位民间艺人表演,其中三人敲锣、击鼓、打钹伴奏,另三人分别扮演狮、佛、猴,后两者手持葵扇、彩巾或青草,围绕狮子的前后左右,用幽默、风趣的形态,做出各种舞姿动作。

Frog-and-Lion in Sanxi, Lechang

Nicknamed Frog Lion, or God Lion,the performance was performed by six to nine folk artistsplaying gong, drum and rattle and three playing the roles of lion, god and monkey. The vivid movements make forextraordinarily funny and interesting performance.

鹤蚌舞

　　取材于翁源民间，表现出动物间应该和睦相处，否则会两败俱伤的哲理，表现出人间向往和平共处的心愿和创造和谐社会的愿望。

Crane and Clam Dance

Originated in Wenyun, it indicates that humans should live harmoniously with the animals.

粤剧

又称"广东大戏",是以梆子、二黄等乐器为主的我国南方一大剧种,是揉合唱做念打、乐师配乐、戏台服饰、抽象形体等的表演艺术。

Yue Opera

It is the major famous opera form in south China based on clappers and Erhuang.

仁化土法造纸

　　流传于广东省韶关市仁化县的一种汉族传统手工技艺，属于土纸制造传统技艺。仁化土纸采用嫩竹做原料，经过选笋、压榨、磋笋、抄纸、切割等大小二十二道工序，人工制作而成。

The Old Way of Paper-Making in Renhua

It is a traditional Han ethnic group way of making paper featured in Shaoguan, Guangdong Province. Tender bamboo stalks are selected, pressed and cut. The paper making process needs to undergo 22 distinct procedures.

剪纸

历史可追溯到六世纪。在创作时，有的用剪子，有的用刻刀，剪纸是一种镂空艺术，在视觉上给人透空的感觉和艺术享受。

Paper Cutting

Paper cutting can be traced back to the 6th century. Both scissors and carving knives are used. It is a "hollow-out" art form.

客家人婚俗

　　始兴的客家人大都是唐宋以后由中原南迁而来的。经过长期与当地土著居民的共同生活，他们的风俗习惯发生了较大变化，既带有中原遗风，又具有当地客家人的印记，特别是婚嫁风俗，更是独具一格、风情万种。

Hakka Wedding Customs

The Hakka people in Shixing originally migrated from the central China plains duringthe Tang (618-907) and Song (960-1279) dynasties. Over time and acculturation with the local people, their customs greatly changed, combining both those of the plain and the locals, making them unique and interesting.

> 客家·回娘家

每年大年初二起至初六，客家妇女会头上戴笠麻，箩格装块冷甜饭，后手中拿柄花布伞，袋里有饭又有肉。

Hakka House · Coming Back to Mother's

Every year from January 2-6 on the lunar calendar, ladies in Hakka put on bamboo hats and return to their mothers' homes with cold sweet rice in their baskets, flowery cloth umbrellas in their hands and rice and meat in their bags.

张田饼印

饼印又称饼模,是生产月饼和各式礼饼的主要工具。张田饼印画面印纹清晰、图案美观大方、线条均匀、立体感强。张田村手艺人先后创作了龙凤伴月、双龙戏珠、寿星麒麟等几十种中秋月饼印和鱼、龟及卡通公仔等一系列礼饼印。

Zhangtian MoonCake Moulds

Also called Moon Cake Impress, it is the main tool for making moon and festival cakes. The mooncake mould in Zhangtian is especially intricate and delicate. Zhangcun craftsmen have accumulateddozens of mooncake and festival cake moulds.

| 趟栊门 |

古老的"防盗门",左右开启。第一道是屏风门,第二道门,叫趟栊门。整个看上去就是一个大的木框,中间横架着十几根圆木。

Tanglong Door

It is an old type burglar resistant door. The first door is the screen; the second is called Tanglong door. It is a large wooden frame with dozens of logs in between.

> 客家·石磨

　　客家人吃的豆腐都是用这个东东磨出来的，磨出来的豆腐细、嫩、滑，现在怀念豆腐里那大自然的气息，所以就怀念石磨了。

Hakka House · Stone Mill
Hakka tofu made by this stone mill is soft, tender and smooth.

打谷子

打谷子是农民一年生产生活中的大事,这种方式已经延续千年。在普遍使用农业现代化机械的今天,粤北地区还有相当多的地方还沿用着这一传统的耕作方式。

Thrashing

Thrashing is a major event for farmers. Used for thousand years, this form is still common in north Guangdong.